The Other Me

(My Moment of Honesty)

James R. Dixon

authorHOUSE®

AuthorHouse™
1663 Liberty Drive
Bloomington, IN 47403
www.authorhouse.com
Phone: 1-800-839-8640

First published by AuthorHouse   3/22/2011

ISBN: 978-1-4567-4325-3 (sc)
ISBN: 978-1-4567-4324-6 (e)

Library of Congress Control Number: 2011903970

Printed in the United States of America

Any people depicted in stock imagery provided by Thinkstock are models, and such images are being used for illustrative purposes only.
Certain stock imagery © Thinkstock.

This book is printed on acid-free paper.

The Other Me was based on what I feel is one of the most important misconceptions about an individual's personality. I'm sure everyone has been perceived in a certain way by others and for the most part those preconceived notions are wrong. With that said, that puts you in the position to have to defend yourself against those who misjudge you. The Other Me poetry book is my self defense. The poems in the book are broken into four sections that determine the makeup of me and my personality. Several misconceptions that were made about me my whole life were that I'm shy, selfish, spiteful, and lazy. The four sections including my love side, emotional side, resilient side, and good side will prove to those who misperceived me that there is more to me than what meets the eye. Those who pry themselves on misjudging others because they are who they are have become my biggest inspiration for the formation of this poetry book. What I hope to accomplish with this book is to give those people in particular a lot more incite as to who I am. The message I would like others to understand from reading this book is not to be afraid of who you are just because someone else doesn't approve. If you have a goal, or dream you would like to achieve don't be afraid to pursue it.

The Love Side of The Other Me is based on a typical love story. You date a woman who is too opposite to be compatible and the relationship takes a turn for the worse. You then say to yourself what were you thinking? Through the mist of the break up process you find a woman who is more your style and you begin to pursue her. One thing leads to another and you then catch deep feelings. Once those events taking place, you eventually fall in love with her.

The Emotional Side of The Other Me explains my take on the way I grew up. Everyone has situations they've encountered such as betrayal, family issues, and personal insecurities. This section of the book goes into details about those things I've experienced and many more.

We then move into the Resilient Side of The Other Me which displays my ability to overcome hardships. A lot of aggression comes out in this section of the book to show my confident attitude. People can relate to me in the sense that everyone has been knocked down before emotionally by another person. But it's how you respond to it that will make you a better person.

The old saying "with pain comes love" brings us to my good side. This section of the book is somewhat self explanatory. I poetically describe some things that make me happy such as living a good lifestyle, providing for myself, and family.

Contents

Resilient Side

Good Side

The Other Me

Love Side

Prima Donna	Diamond
So Emotional	Someone To Love
Girl Like Her	Truth In Love
Tiffany	Kaleidoscope
I Want To Get To Know You	Bleeding Love
Rescue Me	All I Ever Needed
Ready To Fall In Love	

Emotional Side

Quiet Storm	A Place To Call Home II
Just An Old Girlfriend	A Place To Call Home III
Tsunami	World So Bright
Broken Man	World Even Brighter
Abandoned	All I Ever Wanted
Misery of Poverty	
A Place To Call Home I	

Resilient Side

Fear of Flying	Everyone's Third Option
According To You	The Other Me
Invisible	Force of Nature
Things They Say	Open Letter
Speak Now	Let Me Live
Power	Live and Learn

Good Side

Love Side

Prima Donna

After years of pain and heartache
Inflicted upon me by other women
There you stood as the genesis
Of a rejuvenated man
But then disaster struck again
The repeated feeling of being cursed
As your best became your worse
And your true colors were on display
Traveling with you was well
Until I discovered you can't survive
Outside a Ritz Carleton hotel
And the high class life you lead is hell
Manipulating me for material possessions
Seducing me with your body to avoid feeling neglected
Oh the deception, lying, and deceit
You need a thousand dollars worth of accessories
Just to walk down the street
Your Mark Jacobs shades compels men to throttle
Your Prada dresses makes you look like America's top model
Making cases for Jet beauty of the week inside
With Victoria Secret lingerie to show your sexy side
Riding in anything American made is beneath you
You prefer a Mercedes Coupe over my Monte Carlo G2

At the end of the day my logical thinking was out
Being attracted to someone who needs
Five star accommodations just to walk out her house
How meaningless your life has become
Relying on material possessions to help you overcome
The daily pressures and anxiety of life
When your material wishes can be seen on a
Target shelf half priced
Still looking amazing, but you'd rather keep your distance
Because your high maintenance personality
Won't allow you to see the difference
Instantly that doesn't matter anymore
I'm on a search to find true love
So my love life can be restored

So Emotional

You make me feel
So emotional to the point my heart turns blue
Discomforted in my sleep over the thought of losing you
Dreading the waters of which you've walked
My runaway love a distant memory I stalk

You make me cry
Tears of despondency while dying from a broken heart
The light more complicated to contrive in the dark
Tears roll in agony down the edge of my face into a river
Once flowing with your love which made my body shiver

You make me ill
Worrying sick if you will ever come back home
To our affectionate place; without you my desolate heart roams
Waking up every morning to the absence of you
Extinguishes the burning magic created by us two

You make me shy
To interact with other women due to you being my love
Prosperity no longer elevated by your kisses and hugs
You make me feel and cry; You make me ill and shy
My heart is torn into pieces; I'm so emotional inside

Girl Like Her

Stepped out on your wife just to have a rendezvous
With her; you were dying to have her in your life
She was young, confident, sexy, and strong
Fierce walk with a vision of her thong through her skirt
You want a girl like her

She commands attention as she walks down the boulevard
You take her on numerous shopping trips
To bombard her with gifts and take her on trips
You drop your whole bank account in one night on the strip
Because you wanted a girl like her

She craved your attention, but once the funds ran out
She placed you in detention; she's relentless
Got pregnant by another man
But comes back to lead you on again and now your life's ruined
All because you wanted a girl like her

Instead of finding another girl you chase her around the world
When she goes to jail, you're the first to pay her bail
When you fall she kicks you and can care less if you fail
When in need of her most she abandons you and makes your life hell
And it's all because you wanted a girl like her

Senryu Intermission

What must I do
To show you I love you
Men do crazy things for love

To live is to love just as to love is to live.

Tiffany

Miss around the way girl the boys know very well
She makes you fantasize in which your heart melts
With the way she dresses and sexy scent of her Chanel
Indeed you want to stalk her in the mist of where she dwells
The precious smile on her face and green eyes will tell
The story of a beautiful woman wrapped inside a warm shell
5'7 in height and weighs 1,000lbs on the gorgeous scale
Like a painting on the wall of a museum not sold for retail
You can look but can't touch so you continue to sell
The idea of being with her which eventually turns stale
Make several attempts at her, many have tried and failed
So you dream of pursuing her because you have no chance in hell

I Want To Get To Know You

I want to get to know you
I'm sure I will adore you
From watching you rock your hips
And the way you lick your lips

My personal Brittany Spears
That can break me into tears
With words soothing to my soul
Making my heart blush and glow

Your eyes are bright like your smile
Lighting my life for a while
With your soft voice I'm amazed
My mind entering a stage

Of high exhilaration
Passion, lust, and gyration
Your touch hypnotizes me
And makes me feel so elite

To be in your company
And in your arms I feel weak
Destiny rises again
And as sunshine falls I'm in

Rescue Me

For everlasting love
With the mate in your life
Follow this recipe
And love will set you free

Listen
Listen frequently
To your mate as they open up
To you about their life and lets you in their heart

Understand
Understand the circumstance
It's about the bond between the two
Then the emotional connection will shine through

Faith
Have faith
In each other and believe you will
Be able to overcome situations that may tear you apart

Love
Love your mate
Until the end of time for better or worse
Love will be your remedy for an everlasting bond

Senryu Intermission

Love is a process
But love holds no boundaries
Love is a blessing

To know me is to love me so I want you to know me very well.

Ready To Fall In Love

What started as a fantasy
Became more of a fatal attraction
There I was trapped in my box
Ready to fall in love
I'm losing my focus
In case you haven't noticed
The divine touch of your hand
Arouses me like you wouldn't expect it
I was deeply congested
And my heart was breathless
Your like a mural painting on my wall
And there I saw
Me ready to fall in love
The soft touch of your kiss
Against my lips
Had me knocking on your door
At two o' clock in the morning
With a hunger for more
Of your loving and care
And then I would stare
Day dreaming in such a daze
Me caressing your body
Wasn't just a phase

I craved more time with you
Just to hear your voice
I rejoiced making out with you
You had my head spinning
I hope those times
Wouldn't come to an end
But just be a new beginning
Live and learn is all I can do
In the mean time
I'm ready to fall in love with you

Diamond

A
Diamond
Shines bright
Like stars in the night
Like the sunset on the river
Dawning a warm summer night
A diamond is said to be told
Its soothing to the soul
Value good as gold
Surely a glow
Hearts
Go

Someone To Love

Special woman that
Once was my friend who
Means the world to me
Entered my heart
One day and captured my soul
Never giving up on me
Encouraging me to be better
Truly caring and trustworthy
On the day we first met
Loving everything about me
Only to become my true love
Valuable to my life and brings
Everlasting love for eternity

Senryu Intermission

Love is mischievous
When angry seek to be kind
Love for a lifetime

I wondered what I must do to have you. Now that I have you I wonder what I must do.

Truth In Love

You have to understand the truth in love

It's a lot more to it than kisses and hugs

It's about a physical and emotional bond between the two

No matter what you do, you both have to stay true

You're never going to make it, you're too different is what they say

Stand by each other through thick and thin is the rule love made

Instead of telling the world, you rather live inside out

By keeping it among the two of you hoping nobody finds out

You have to understand the truth in love

It's a lot more to it than kisses and hugs

One can get possessive and claim everything's all mine

The other will get mad and threaten not to be there through hard times

You have to develop the attitude of never say die

Just the very thought of it makes you both want to cry

The make-ups after fights helps the relationship last longer

Whatever doesn't kill you definitely makes you stronger

You have to understand the truth in love

It's a lot more to it than kisses and hugs

It takes a lot of time, hard work, patience, and devotion

To form a lasting commitment with little commotion

You have to agree that what's mine is yours and what's yours is mine

Then and only then will everything work out fine

You have to work together and I can't preach it enough

Just to understand the truth in love

Kaleidoscope

When I looked into your eyes for the first time
I saw my future speaking to me inside
I instantly hugged you with no hesitation
Impatiently waiting for my southern region to enter your loving nation
The very thought of making love to you gave me good vibrations
The answer to the question quickly led to masturbation
Anticipating my feelings and emotions through your presentation
Dreams of your divine touch causing my exasperation
The day we performed was filled with blissful restoration
Of my bipolar mood swings relieving my desperation
The room filled with aphrodisiac like decorations
Had me moaning aloud sexual declarations
My hearts skipping and bloods racing from sexual captivation
Giving me a liberated feeling that I've reached heavenly destination
When I looked into your eyes for the first time
I saw my future speaking to me inside

Senryu Intermission

Love can be heartfelt
Love can be pleasure and pain
Love can be passion

Love turns what once was a fore-thought in fantasy into reality. Love has a voice and it speaks loudly.

Bleeding Love

Amid ocean front my heart stands pleading love;
Into misty skies my heart lusts bleeding love.

Contemplating the voice of the one I love transcending love
As waters wash against the shores of exceeding love.

My impassioned heart soaring atop a mountain,
With glacial stones carved with words of my soul reading love.

Her compassion and benevolent acts soothe me
As my heart accelerates down a highway of speeding love.

Above all the rest I stand delighted
With my heart and soul in unison voicing succeeding love.

All I Ever Needed

There I lay feeling blue
Visioning images on the
Vaulted ceiling of you
Reminiscing the highs
And the lows
Thinking you were the one
Who would be with me as
I grew old
I needed your hand
To hold on to
The storm that nearly tore
Us apart you pulled me through
I needed your heart
To hold on to
All I ever needed was you

I treasured our first date
Along with our first kiss
The connections our hearts made
I hoped would never end
The promises we made were true
As you stood by me
And I stood by you
We shared joy, tears, and pain
Those times I wished would never change
In your arms I felt safe with you
As I recap the pain I went through
My heart cries for you
All I ever needed was you

The trips we've been taking
Healed all the heartbreaking
One person who would
Understand me is all I've longed for
With you the risk was low
With a high reward
Spending my time with you
Turned out to be a dream come true
We didn't need fortune and fame
And although we've acquired it
Our lives still stayed the same
As I recap the pain I went through
My heart cries for you
I needed your heart
To hold on to
All I ever needed was you

Emotional Side

Quiet Storm
Just An Old Girlfriend
Tsunami
Broken Man
Abandoned
Misery of Poverty
A Place To Call Home I
A Place To Call Home II
A Place To Call Home III
World So Bright
World Even Brighter
All I Ever Wanted

Quiet Storm

Heavy rains and storms made it hard for her to see
A young woman's life was taken away every hope and dream
It seems her life was altered after the night
She lost her virginity once her vagina was stroked
Her student accolades were the best, she then became a victim
Of emotional distress due to her peers ostracizing her
She wished she would've rescinded that night like a false alarm
Now she's in the emergency room with ivies in her arm
No longer able to accept her scholarship at Princeton
Along with that she forfeited her prom, grad night, and high school education
Now all she does is recap her childhood as her belly gets bigger
Future modeling and acting career gone due to loss of her figure
She had her life mapped out, but not once did she see this
One morning at dawn crying to God I'm not ready for a kid
Diapers, toys, formula, bottles, and clothes
She lost her job so with no income her hearts about to explode
Now she has to rely on her parents and other people she's related
Because her baby's father is out getting intoxicated
While on bed rest she instantly gets mad as she looks out the window
To see her friends living the life she once had
As a teen mom her life was set back and had to restart up
To prevent this from happening to you wrap it up
Or don't do it at all and you won't have to worry
Because your baby having a baby, don't be in such a hurry

Just An Old Girlfriend

My perception of our reality together seemed real

After a month it was all over my time was wasted and killed

The stress you placed upon me led to many sleepless nights

Why did I let you tear me up inside? You're just an old girlfriend!

You disrespected me and trashed me repeatedly

I removed you from my life due to flashbacks of how you treated me

You promised, but never changed every time I gave you a try

Why did I let you tear me up inside? You're just an old girlfriend!

After a week together you told me I was your finest

Rather than do right by me; you took advantage of my kindness

When you called me your best friend I thought you were drunk inside

Why did I let you tear me up inside? You're just an old girlfriend!

Being with you was a challenge; after a week I should've quit

The emotional damage you inflicted made me feel relationships aren't worth it

Why get married during the day with the chance of a divorce at night

Why did I let you tear me up inside? You're just an old girlfriend!

Senryu Intermission

Look into my eyes
Tell me if you think or see
The soul of a man

They say no matter how bad your life is there's always someone else who has it worse. However I don't think that applies to me sometimes.

Tsunami

I once thought
Money was the root of all evil
Until I met her
The storm that would change
My life for the worse
The fire that would burn down
What took years to build
The burst of water
That would drown what I stood
And lived for
Leaving nothing left for me
But memories of my misery
Along with the feeling of being
Trapped inside a cage
Filled with rage from the pain
That was bestowed upon me
How will I rise
Is it possible for me to be refurbished
Or will my remains
Be made a monument
For my loved ones to reminisce

Broken Man

All I see is a broken man
Emotionally damaged
Physically decimated
Struck by the pressures of life
His strength quickly diminished
Here lays a broken man

All I see is a broken man
Disconsolate spirits
Demented soul
Striped of his livelihood
His confidence rapidly liquidated
Here lays a broken man

All I see is a broken man
Flared temperament
Ferocious attitude
Tormented by his family
His patience instantly defunct
Here lays a broken man

All I see is a broken man
Mentally distraught
Vision impaired
Hopes and dreams shattered
His life quickly stunned
Here lays a broken man

Abandoned

Shattered dreams at an early age
Ceilings crashing down, walls closing in
Young boy isolated by his family
Sad, but half of them couldn't stand him
Woke up one morning all alone
Walked around the house, family was all gone
Made several calls no one answered their phones
Then realized he's a victim of a broken home
He sat on the porch crying
Dazed in a frantic panic
Pacing up and down the street
Just to understand he had been abandoned
He questioned why his mother had him
Haunted by visions of his obnoxious father
He prayed the verbal attacks would stop soon
He begged his parents to put him up for adoption
At times he wished he was never born
Because his heart was constantly getting torn
His father broke him into tears until his head was damp
While his mother threatened to send him to juvenile camp
Eventually the young boy broke free
Developed street smarts and learned how to be
Independent to the finish to give life another try
Because the first thought on his mind was this can't be life

Misery of Poverty

He grew up in poverty and hunger
Questioning where his next meal would come from
Surviving the day is what he'd wonder
Laying scared for starvation to be done
His world became hopeless, bleak, and somber
Awaiting for change and Jesus to come
To instill him with confidence and strength
With the rebirth of his new commencement

Through bricolage he tried to build a home
But winds of the cold dark night were too strong
As he saw his home vacated and stoned
All he's lived for and memories were gone
He claimed he felt less pain having no home
The bleeding of his heart wasn't so long
He felt dead, hopeless, lifeless, and breathless
Praying the day he'll be resurrected

Senryu Intermission

Isolation is formed by
The want of independence
For one self

In a world full of so many chiefs and Indians stands a lone wolf in the mist of the darkness.

A Place To Call Home I

At a day in age my life went up in the air

It was that particular moment I realized life isn't fair

At one point in time under one roof, it was four of us strong

Then one dies, it was three left, how could we all get along

I took that as my que to be different

Never walked down the same road as you which is why I never did fit in

I was excluded from your plans so I walked on my own

Being criticized for everything I've done until I was grown

You all slandered me constantly; every other word was a diss

And had the nerve to mistake my non-existence for selfishness

We were supposed to raise each other to make life nice and free

I never questioned you on who you are, but it's a shame you did it to me

Most arguments led to physical actions which had me confused

Always losing your patience and the result was I got abused

How did I stand for this anger and tolerate this pain for so long

I guess it made me stronger in the end as I'm soon to be gone

I never realized what I wanted was too much to ask for
I feel like I'm being pushed and pulled back and forth
As I live and dream I fear that I'll live life alone
I'm destined to find a place to call home

A Place To Call Home II

I wish I could say no more crying, but things still hurt

I try to forget about bad times, but can't help but be disturbed

It's a shame you wasn't there to witness some of my first

Sometimes I feel you don't exist in which I'm at a loss of words

I try to see things your way and all I get is a blatant stare

I rarely hear from you once a week and you still claim that you care

How can you teach me to be a man, you never gave me anything you never had

And it's sad how you dumped all your responsibilities on your dad

It's bad that when you speak all people do is doubt you

It's sad that you have three kids that don't really care about you

You claim you're here to help me, but I don't believe a word you say

Broken promises over the years cause you to lie everyday

When I was younger I couldn't look at you without shedding a few tears

Now that I'm grown, no more intimidation, and no fear

You're dismantled in your own misery so you take it out on me

You never supported or respected me, but in due time you'll need me

I never realized what I wanted was too much to ask for
I feel like I'm being pushed and pulled back and forth
As I live and dream I fear that I'll live life alone
I'm destined to find a place to call home

A Place To Call Home III

Most of my time is spent asking questions that drag me

Like why weren't my parents better prepared to have me

I'm convicted of a broken home because they were both out splurging

Some mornings I wake up feeling like I don't have a purpose

My parents never made amends and till this day they hate each other

Leaving me broke and decrepit feeling like I have no sisters or brothers

So I stick to myself and as I hook up my space

I'm visioning plans of action for my chance to get away

My guardian drives me crazy, my time with her will soon finish

She never respected my mind state; I've always had an objective opinion

I disagreed with nearly every word that came out of her mouth

I never once kissed up to her so she threatened to kick me out of her house

As I rebel against the hate I will stay alive and survive

You can't kill my spirit and faith no matter how hard you try

I don't believe those who say they're here for me; I've heard it all before

So I rely on God to provide the light as I open the door

I never realized what I wanted was too much to ask for
I feel like I'm being pushed and pulled back and forth
As I live and dream I fear that I'll live life alone
I'm destined to find a place to call home

Senryu Intermission

Everyone's in need of
A place to call home
For comfort, warmth, and love

Independent souls who don't pander to the minions usually aren't welcomed into the home of their leader. Rather than follow, they find their own inner sanctum.

World So Bright

So many sleepless nights, I stayed up thinking about
How my life would've been had I stayed out drinking
I'm just trying to establish a presence
I look at those around me and feel I'm fighting so I don't end up like them
It's such a sad story for those who have no restraint
Some use people to get over while others file a complaint
And yes society is different
I put my heart and soul in my work every day to get away from it
It's funny how everyone has suggestions for me to do
Just because you don't have what it takes you want me to be like you
No one lets me walk my own way
As I live I dream of being one with God and carrying out my space
As I walk through another day in my life
I recap the moments that I stood up to fight
So much pain to a life makes it hard to see the light
I'm focused on opening up a world so bright

World Even Brighter

Some ask me why I have more struggles than good times
Try living life alone, how hard is it to unwind
Me and my parents had beef with each other
My dad never taught me to be a man and left that responsibility to my brothers
However they never did a good job in my mind
They struggled in their own lives so how could they help me with mine
I felt like I was tossed to the wolves
I went through physical abuse at home and emotional abuse at school
My dad wants me to be a follower and I don't understand why I should
That leaves me with a blank stare on my face feeling misunderstood
Now those who made me shy to speak
Are coming back trying to take credit for my success and be a part of my speech
As more opportunities knock the doors close tighter
Its hard to envision the doors of success opening wider
The emotion is hard although the work is much lighter
I'm focused on opening up a world even brighter

All I Ever Wanted

All I ever wanted was to be accepted
But I felt I was tried and tested
And under the pressure I showed you my worse

All I ever wanted was to be loved
But I felt I was pushed and shoved
Out of the way of the golden child so I rebelled

All I ever wanted was a place to call home
But I felt I was grown and shown
Unorthodox methods to receive and achieve that goal

In the future I won't be so blind
When angry I will seek to be kind
Try to be divine and finally find
That place to call home which is all I ever wanted

Resilient Side

Fear of Flying
According To You
Invisible
Things They Say
Speak Now
Power
Everyone's Third Option
The Other Me
Force of Nature
Open Letter
Let Me Live
Live and Learn

Fear of Flying

He had to go when not ready to leave
His insufficient answers scared him dry
He feared failure and refused to believe
He had what it took to give it a try
While Inspired to dream he'd receive
The strength of God to spread his wings and fly
To a destination of peace and love
Living free like the releasing of doves

From his intimidation he broke free
A new confident soaring eagle flies
His dreams became reality indeed
You see his name in lights as he arrives
From that lonely place as he can now breathe
And see how his creations came to life
The complete shock and awe was developed
Soon his family and peers became star struck

According To You

According to you, I'm a waste of sperm and life
I have no personality; I'm too uptight
Having talent is worthless if it's not in sight
According to you, I can't do anything right

Little do you see, I am an endangered species
I write the truth for those afraid and shy to speak
My words lethally inject the minds of the weak
Creating images for those blind and can't see

According to you, I'm difficult and lazy
I don't strive to achieve goals and I'm too hasty
I don't do what I preach, or hear what's said to me
According to you, I've disgraced those who made me

Little do you see, I've turned water into wine
With creations so divine they ease your mind
Laying waste to non believers on my own time
Proving that I'm everything you're not and can't find

Senryu Intermission

My unspoken thoughts
Have illustrated the path
Of my destiny

If I follow the advice of the idiotic ones I will get nowhere in life as opposed to following the advice of the most dominating source.

Invisible

The quiet ones have the most to say
It's getting others to hear them that's the problem
They close themselves off to the free world
In hopes that one day someone will listen

The quiet ones get the least attention
Because others are threatened by their zeal
They don't act out of their character to get noticed
In life they're more at peace within themselves

The quiet ones are the most ostracized
It's getting others to renege on the scrutiny that's the problem
They feel invisible to the free world
In society they're the most resilient and valued

Things They Say

Although the sky is clear it still pours down rain

                                                        One look in the clouds I see the things they say

Your poetry is meager and mindsets feeble

                                                         Like defected wings of a soaring eagle

You lack creative energy; please just stop

                                              You don't have what it takes and your books will flop

Consider finding a new line of work kid,

                                              You're just not good enough, or cut out for this

I'm not one to listen, or change profiles

                                              After careful thought I then changed my style

My creative energy was soon restored

                                       Proving those wrong who once thought my work was bored

Now find themselves reciting my work at dawn

                                              Making me a new poetry phenomenon

As the rain thins out, the sky becomes more clear

                                              No clouds in the sky, but my work you can hear

Speak Now

The misperception placed upon me is that I'm quiet.
I'm the health care here to put them on a diet.
My destiny exceeds farther than what they can see.
Their vision is impaired by sexual and alcohol obscurity.
Their judgments are welcome;
It's hilarious how the moronic ones have the most meaningless
things to say.
It's as if an undertaker was called to bury the brains of
the unintelligent.
Their judgments are like verbal ailments in which
they should be hospitalized.
It seems their mentally brain washed and trapped inside
their own misery.
I cheat those who would rather have me be less than what I am.
I don't deal well with fake people.
Those who smile in my face, but talk about me behind my back.
You're spineless, feeble, and meager.
Break free of your insecurities and get over yourself.
They say speak now, or forever hold your peace.
So I'm here to speak out to those who misperceive me.

Senryu Intermission

Those who mistake
Confidence for cockiness
Aren't truly confident

The insecure ones are quick to accuse the confident ones of being cocky because they wish they possessed the confidence they have.

Power

It's crazy how a black man can have so much power
It's in the tongue from every minute to every hour
Sad to say, but till this day it still continues
Racial depravity oppressing society isn't new

You accuse us of being lazy, but what's the translation
You're egotistic because you've received higher education
There's a higher success rate of you than us; don't be so optimistic
We're capable of Masters Degree earnings check the tax bracket

Some of us make more hourly than you make quarterly
You're so close-minded that you can't solve problems in orderly
Fashion because you're arrogant while simultaneously ignorant
Assuming our kids will be failures if we impregnate a white woman

For years you were the abomination of the black nation
It was said that our independence was the reason for your hatred
Accusing us of an obsession for material wishes that entices stagflation
Or was it our creativity to invent a new language

Why else would you be mad I have countless reasons
Don't be so immature and find reconciliation
Are you racially free inside your mind
Or do you wish you were black on the inside

Everyone's Third Option

There's a thin line to distinguish the real from the fake
It's getting thinner with peoples actions being fraudulent
They pretend to want you around so they can take
Advantage of the soon to be forgotten spirit
Some of mankind chooses reputation over self confidence
Independence is absent which in society makes them a peasant

With that said that only leaves me two roads
When everyone drifted right I turned left
I'm a product of my maker and my individuality continues to mold
You're a follower who applauds the amputation of your self-respect
Then you expect me to follow in your footsteps thinking it's right
You're a wolf in sheep's clothing whose afraid to see the light

A little over two decades of isolation and exclusion
During that time I was reluctant, but fortunate to see
The fake and hate in people as if it were a mental contusion
They're suffering from a disease called envy along with greed
Your life has become predictable with no originality
While I'm a non artificial leader enhancing my formality

The Other Me

I plan to write a poetry book and the feedback I received hurt
Get real is what they told me; how would that work?
What would you talk about? What audience can you capture?
You're a quiet spirit caught up in your own rapture
You being a social outcast would work against you
You would suffer disappointment and embarrassment too
Don't quit your day job as you will need it at night
Because the chance of you pulling this off is not quite

BUT

The other me can care less what you think
I'm confident in my abilities and my faith will set me free
What sets me free and apart from losers like you is my reality
Half of you live in fantasies and the other half takes a back seat
I'm in the driver's seat taking control of my destiny
Whereas you're a desperate house wife living off your mates money
So please continue to count me out and you'll see the difference
As I sprout from the underground with a vengeance

Senryu Intermission

I will not stop
You can try to slow me down
But I'll rise to the top

If you think for one second you have the power to make me feel as weak as the ones you have made in the past with your demonstrative mindset, think again. I'm not the one.

Force of Nature

Sometimes I feel like no one cares to understand my pain
They either take me as a joke, or they think it's a game
To dismantle my humanity; which would deem them insane
My actions would be hazardous to their egos and coerce them to take blame

Although its picture perfect, I don't paint a perfect picture
Nor do I see anybody, but haters and gold diggers
Who viewed me as unimportant since the day of my birth
They left me for dead in hopes I would drop off the face of the earth

The disappointing part about it is the fact that I'm still here
Willing to be the most hated and the one they all fear
The person they all hear, the burning that makes them shed tears
The toxic that makes their heads weird, America's worst nightmare

The power of poetry has been instilled in me so get used to this
My words can levitate your body and mind by way of telekinesis
For those who despise me; understand I am a chosen one
But what will make your soul sick is the fact that I just begun

I am an artist
I am a force of nature

Open Letter

What more should I do? How much do I give?
How do I breathe? How can I live?
How can I see? Where do I go from here?
When is my coming? How will it steer?
Constantly trying to live up
To everyone's expectations in the dark
To avoid further pain and
Excavation to the heart
As if the pressure wasn't enough
With everything and everyone gone
I'm understanding all of my rights
And where I went wrong
So I'm writing you this letter
In the form of a song
Asking for your helping hand
Please don't leave me alone
I want to grow as a person and learn
You're the one who can teach it to me
In the end you will see
A nice future with the new and improved me

Senryu Intermission

Your distractions mean nothing
I'm done with leaning on trees
With fake leaves

Let me live without your alternatives, or you telling me how to live. After all, your life is pathetic to the point of no return. So get you some business and stay out of mine.

Let Me Live

Not in many years did I envision my life
Happening this way, take a look in my eyes
Feel the determination of a man insane
Who under attack stands like a soldier through rain

Let me live; Let me dream
Let me learn; Let me ask

I'm a survivor in this world against all odds
I went from an outcast to a solo star
They questioned my decisions as if they were unintelligent
My lashing out was through poetic justified dominance

Let me breathe; Let me see
Let me feel; Let me say

Relationships impeccable despite malevolent people
Controlling headstrong women overstepping their boundaries
I maintain a humble attitude the best way I could
They leave me misunderstood although my intentions are good

Let me love: Let me smile
Let me work; Let me laugh

Live and Learn

To live successfully
Create a plan to survive
Follow this recipe
To form a beautiful life

Live
Live everyday
As if it were your last
Make quality moves and good decisions fast

Grow
Grow emotionally
Develop a competitive spirit
And your emotional advantage others will see

Teach
Teach yourself
Mentoring skills to create a novelty
Portray a confident attitude through positivity

Learn
Learn intangibles
Assets that can never be taught
Then the once hard battle becomes easily fought

Good Side

In My Element
I Don't See Anybody
My World, My Way
There Is No Competition
Pass The Torch
Revolutionize Me
Wasting Time
Recipe For Happiness
The Good Life
No Better Love
Walk of Life
Bigger Picture
Poetry Invasion

In My Element

As I step on the scene in Gucci green
Living the life I once planned, hoped, and dreamed
Heads turn at the reciting of a poem
Audiences join to form poetry zones

A hostile takeover comes in action
As inspired poets form their factions
Healing a world that is injury prone
Audiences join to form poetry zones

A world once torn is reborn through poetry
As poets let their publications speak
A revived world creates lavish homes as
Audiences join to form poetry zones

As I step on the scene in Gucci green
Audiences join to form poetry zones

I Don't See Anybody

As I look from a far I see there is no competition
It's just me, my inner circle, and the plan for my vision
I envision me atop a mountain starring down on my abominate people
Those who belittled me are watching my success from a steep hole

Indiscriminate souls find their way to me on a day to day
Others have their views on my topics, but I express them in a valiant way
Not afraid of the criticism, or unfavorable attention I may receive
Regardless of all that success is still what I achieve

I'm a student to the arts, but poetry isn't new to me
I treat my poetry like my wife and make love to it fluently
Indescribable sounds emerge due to the sensibility of my poems
And the sovereignty to turn poems into letters and songs

I don't see anybody; maybe they just don't shine bright
But in order to see me you'll need a stage light
After reading this maybe your lack of attention will decrease
And your abominated mindset will soon be deceased

Senryu Intermission

It's hard to imagine failure
When you're on top
Of the world non stop

Take your place in the game immediately. If you procrastinate there is always someone else ready to take your spot.

My World, My Way

My world my way! Where have I heard that before?
That once was the cardinal sin I was forced to live in
Who made you the chairman of my success and plots
You don't dictate when it starts and stops and it's not over

You should feel ashamed; at one point you disowned me
Now that glory is rolling in you want to act like you know me
Phony you are; a mere shell of a man
Me on the other hand I'm a man; a proven man
As I stand on my own two feet in the sand
Taking a stand; like a 757 when I land
Evacuate your plan; they've immediately been abandoned
Let the man in the sand draw a line to your fate

My world my way! Where have I heard that before?
From the enraged lion at the front of the zoo door
Who is willing to endure; more pain and punishment to the core
Because in the outcome his image will be restored

There Is No Competition

After four divorces, no career, or stability
You have the nerve to compete with me
It's like walking into a world war
With no supplies, or weaponry
You see your life on a big screen
Now try to compare it to mine
It's embarrassing what you've done
The lackluster of opportunities you left behind
Why was it hard for you to be there for me
Your legacy was tainted
Due to the corruption of your humanity
I defended you against those who verbally taunted you
During my leave of absence you insulted me
Concluding with me being dumb, stupid, and irrelevant
Mistaking me for what you are and making incoherent judgments
But look at me now on top of the world without you
And a message for those who didn't know the real you
You've been bamboozled and hoodwinked
By the acts and words of a selfish man
Who's to cocky to understand
That the world doesn't revolve around him
Rather than be vengeful I move on gracefully
Non antagonistic staying peaceful and serene
I'm relieved of stress and enjoying my success
My revolution of distress exist no more
As I live the good life in the open floor

Pass The Torch

Through the unification of my assets
I started a poetry epidemic.
I took it global whereas most people
wouldn't make it outside their mother's kitchen.
They just sit on the porch and read
their poetry to grandma,
while I'm hosting seminars
around the world nonstop.
I'm educating communities preventing
them from systematically crumbling.
The significance of your poems are
like alcoholics, their stumbling.
Readers wondering if your points
are made clear; wanting to throw
a spear threw your collection
because the insignificance of your message
overlooks the value of its worth.
In case you're misunderstanding exactly
what I'm saying; pass the torch to someone
who cares because what you're doing is dangerous.
You're only trying to become famous, but the
art is thicker. While I'm burping poetry
like it's my baby and I'm its father figure.
This is my heart and soul.
This is my life and everything I own.
So stop poisoning it with your irrelevance
and allow it to be grown.

Senryu Intermission

Never give up
Don't hold back
Have faith in yourself
Keep your goals in tact

Never give anyone power over you. If you have people in your life who thinks what you're doing is wrong, ask them what are they doing and/or what have they done for themselves? Most likely it isn't anything significant.

Revolutionize Me

Revoke the labels placed upon me from
External sources whose opinions don't mean anything
Virtually I see how people operate
Only under the influence of someone else
Likely to be inebriated inside, but I'm
Utilized for my strengths which continuously builds and
Transformation is in heavy rotation while
Infection was removed from the emotional incline
Or if you're still in disbelief
Notice how I constantly flourish and
Inspire those around me to be better by the
Zeal that I possess and my fortitude is
Extremely immaculate forcing the weak to
Modify their strategy to out shine this
Everlasting poet who is determined to be noticed

Wasting Time

Stop… take a minute to listen, envision
Understand and witness the position you're in
Life is hard, you don't always get what you want
Times are hard, no supplies, or food on the table this month

Today marks the day of a new journey; no more excuses
I refuse to be held captive from my past
So I'd rather be an architect of my future
By perfecting my craft so it flows like fluid

It's hard to believe you tried to discourage me
From fulfilling my destiny, hopes, and dreams
And it is you who entices me to erupt and write
Vigorous poems for haters like you to shut you up

My writing has evolved into another dimension
That would allow me to release tension and as mentioned
I speak the truth that would propose me an extension
Of another manuscript like a second dimension

I'm just trying to free my mind
Trying to find some peace of mind
It's not like I'm wasting time
Or throwing away my life

Recipe For Happiness

Live life nice and free
Don't let your happenings
Destroy your happiness

Life is what you make it
Don't mourn the bad
Be thankful for the good times

Don't wait tomorrow
What you can do today
Don't sleep your life away

Exercise your body
Mind and soul to
Create your own happiness

Senryu Intermission

Success is a virtue
If you believe in it
You can achieve it

Educate yourself in your field of expertise. The more knowledge you have equals the higher advantage you're going to have over your competitors.

The Good Life

All I've been working for is my piece of the good life
Along with someone to share it with in the form of a good wife
Reality has set in as I've awaken from my narcissistic stage
Awaiting for my dreams to become reality before I age

Dolce and Gabbana shades as I drive through the town
In a Lexus with a King James license plate atop a gold plated crown
Red Lincoln MKZ for the winter and an H2 Hummer
A muscular body with six pack abs to show off in the summer

A Victorian residence to reside in fabulous living
With a brass water fountain raining Kool-Aid for my children
Marble floors and countertops with suede couches under me
Watching the Lakers on a 75 inch flat screen

Taking family vacations in some of the world's hottest spots
Or partying on a yacht the size of a city block
Dining in Hollywood for breakfast and New York City for dinner
Flying via private jet through the summer and winter

Insurmountable bank account minus the price of fame
Living large with three homes, four cars, and five names
I can be James Jackson, Grant, or James Franklin
The good life is a blessing and in due time I'll live it

No Better Love

All this time I spent searching
Ended up being a waste of my time
As you were right in front of my face
Rather than my distant mind
True love like you is hard to find
Now that I found you I want to make you mine
You inspire me to be a better man
You release my pain through the singing of your band
But you allow me to create the music
Once you gave me your love I never abused it
Instead I used it to my advantage
To eradicate my hard times so they would vanish
You provided the home I now stay in
Your smile and grace gave me an arena to play in
Welcoming me with open arms with your glory
You've become my blank canvas that allows me to tell a story
I pray daily that I can keep you in my life
I now nominate you my personal guiding light
You're hotter than the sun which would blind my sights
My sunshine; carry me to paradise
We can leave the world behind and yes its true
My girlfriend is jealous of the bond I have with you
But I'm ready to commit to you
After all, you serve as medication when my heart is blue

I knew my relationship with her wouldn't last
I want you to be my future; I'm over my past
Rather than stress me you caress me
I love the way you test me to get the best of me
They say there's someone for everyone
And I know you're the one for me
There's no denying that you prove it to me
Through the power of your poetry
Or is that me saying thanks for giving me space to say
When others left me you never ran away
I won't be blinded again, or make the same mistake
To have you in my life I greatly appreciate

Walk of Life

Why don't you take a minute from star gazing
To realize what you have is amazing
A son who ended up setting the bar for you
To live up to in which you should be embracing
You have your father to thank
For taking care of your responsibilities
When in need of a father figure he was there for me
To serve as a role model for me and also to you
You claimed I didn't have a pot to piss in
Well neither did you
As your father took care of you
Until you were fifty-two
But I didn't need you to take care of me
As my mother played both mother and father to me
Because you were deployed to a concentration camp
Along with other fathers who had become dead beats
It's easy to get caught up in being selfish to me
You had others fooled, but you weren't fooling me
As I saw right through you for who you really are
A cheap, selfish, lying bastard who never made it far
When confronted you were ready to kick me to the curb
Here I am thinking you're a man and it's not true; it's a shame
You put up a bigger fight over a woman who doesn't want you

Academy award for the biggest loser goes to you
I hope it's nice for you to have your American honey
After all, you would sell your family up the river for money
I was blessed to have broken free of your custody
I can't imagine where I would've been had you raised me
The thought of it alone gives me nightmares
Dripping in a cold sweat and shedding tears
I guess I chose the right walk of life
In the end will things ever be right

Senryu Intermission

To fill the vision
Of my fantasy
The good life is what I need

Palm trees, ninety degrees, lounging with my family, feeling the cool summer breeze. The good life sounds good to me.

Bigger Picture

I feel like I'm standing on the edge of a cliff
With no fear of falling
Or stalling on being the best I can be
Working hard has become a lifestyle for me
They're looking at me like success came easily
Don't let your pride be your own worst enemy
In order to create your own success
Be confident and strong
Be dedicated to whatever it is you're doing
Whether it's sports, medicine, or writing a song
Take a stand for yourself
Let no one tell you what you're doing is wrong
If they laugh in your face
You should laugh harder
Because they're wishing they were where you are
And while your succeeding they're just getting started
Pretty soon all the laughing will stop
They will embrace you in the end
Once they see themselves in the loser circle
As you continue to win

Take it from me
Someone who has been mocked before
Taken as a joke by his family and friends
Now they come to me wanting more
Like never before so the story never ends
Separate your real friends from the fake
Realize the talents you have and what's at stake
Don't take for granted the talent you've been given
Proceed with no fear
And the good life you'll be living

Poetry Invasion

The first day of the rest of my life
Was haunted by blurry visions at night
My spirit mauled by multiple attacks
Physically and emotionally ruined my heart sat
Suddenly desperation swiftly came to an end
Innumerable phrases began to metamorphose me inside
The magnitude of self expression making my body unwind
With dynamic words expediting the enhancement of my mind
The ability to create and articulate a thesis
Brought indulgence to my soul like you wouldn't believe it
The laughter it brings along with the pain that it sings
Administers a comforting feeling like the wind beneath my wings
Poetry invaded my soul and rendered me unconscious
Like an angel in my dream acknowledging my invocation
Every step I take and every breath I breathe
I will live, eat, and sleep poetry

To veteran artists,

We must continue to perfect our craft to better the arts. We uphold many positions, but our main position is to inspire the youth to want to achieve more in their lives. We can do this by portraying the right message. If we show them that we have what it takes to maintain our craft and continuously get better, then we have achieved that goal. It is important for us to share any knowledge and wisdom about the particular works of art we are pursuing so we can help to get them involved. After all, they won't know how far they can go unless we show them where we've been. So in the future, continue to set an example for the youth and other upcoming artists to follow. Be an example and not a demonstration.

James R. Dixon

To aspiring artists,

Have faith in your work especially when no one has faith in you. Don't be afraid of what you do and what your work represents. Be confident that others will pick up on the message you're trying to send. Do the research on other artists who came before you and their journey to success. That will help you to determine where you want to take your work. It also draws inspiration. Put yourself in a position to inspire another person to pursue different forms of art so you can be a part of the rebuilding process. Be an example and not a demonstration.

James R. Dixon

I want to give a special thank you to everyone for taking time out of your busy schedules to ponder my thoughts and gain more knowledge about me as a person. I hope you found some of my likes and dislikes interesting to say the least. My main concern was the message I wanted to send with this first manuscript. So as long as someone picked up on the message, my mission has been accomplished. There are many more manuscripts where this came from so if The Other Me has interested you in any way, be on the lookout for future projects.

James Dixon

I was born and raised in San Bernardino County, California. I grew up from humble beginnings in a single parent home. With no father around, my mother managed to raise three children on her own. I began writing when I was in junior high school. I took creative writing classes in high school and began learning more about poetry. I was told I have a future in poetry writing after reciting a few poems for several acquaintances at that time. While in college, the two English classes I've taken helped to develop my writing skills. I looked at poetry writing as a form of expressing my views on multiple topics. It then became my voice and a great way for me to be creative. The Other Me is my first manuscript and we will all be witnesses to see where this goes from here.